# The Mighty Murray

Written by
Patrick Lay and Joshua Hatch

Flying Start
to Literacy®

T0363466

# Contents

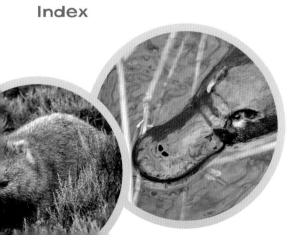

# Introduction

There is just one thing every single living organism on Earth needs to survive: water. Without water, there is no life on Earth. Many organisms also need other things: sunlight, oxygen, certain vitamins and minerals; but every single living thing on this planet requires water.

Rivers are important. The fresh water they bring inland from mountain springs and snowmelt is what makes life on land possible – from wildlife to agriculture to our own human existence. Water is life.

A satellite image of Australia

Australia is one of the driest places on Earth. More than 20 per cent of Australia is considered desert. Think about all of the people who live in Australia – where do they get their water? One of the main sources of water is the mighty Murray River.

# Where does the Murray flow?

There's a little spot in the wooded mountains on the border between Victoria and New South Wales, near Kosciuszko National Park that doesn't look very special. It just seems like a quiet place to pitch a tent and relax in the bush. But, this spot **is** special – this is where the Murray River starts.

When the snow in this area melts, water seeps into the ground and flows into small streams. These streams run downhill, joining together to form bigger streams and, eventually, rivers.

Kosciuszko National Park

This is how the Murray starts its 2,500-kilometre journey from the southeastern part of Australia to South Australia. It then connects to a series of lakes that eventually drain into the Southern Ocean.

Along the way, other rivers run off from the Murray or join up with it. In fact, the Murray River system includes six of Australia's seven longest rivers, including the Darling River.

### Did you know?

The three longest **navigable** rivers in the world are the Nile, the Amazon and – you guessed it – the Murray.

# The Murray–Darling Basin

The Murray River supports a large area known as the Murray–Darling Basin. This area includes not just the Murray, but dozens of smaller rivers, creeks and streams. Together, this network of rivers provides water to a million square kilometres of land in southeastern Australia. More than two million people and hundreds of species of wildlife call this area home.

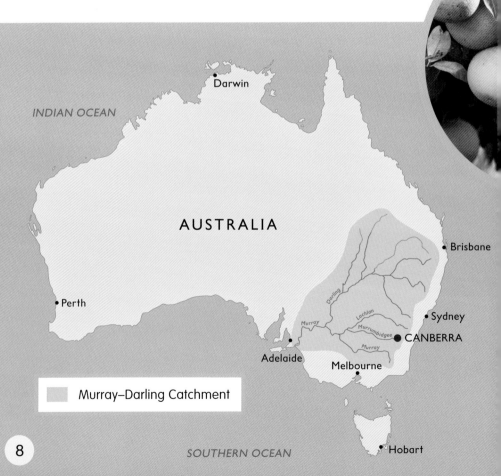

INDIAN OCEAN

• Darwin

AUSTRALIA

• Perth

• Brisbane

Darling

Lachlan

Murray

Murrumbidgee

• Sydney

● CANBERRA

Murray

Adelaide •

Melbourne •

Murray–Darling Catchment

• Hobart

SOUTHERN OCEAN

In this region, 40 per cent of Australia's food is grown, as well as crops such as cotton. Think about this: almost half of the food on your plate – and maybe the clothes you are wearing – were made possible thanks to the Murray River!

# Who lives along the Murray?

A diverse and abundant variety of plants and animals has made the Murray a good home for many people.

## Indigenous peoples

For more than 40,000 years, Indigenous Australian peoples, such as the Bangerang and the Ngarrindjeri, have called the Murray home. But they didn't actually call it the "Murray" – that was the name given to the river by white Europeans when they came to Australia over 200 years ago. Indigenous peoples called the river Murrundi, Millewa, Tongala or Indi, depending on the part of the river where they lived.

The Murray had an abundance of fish. Indigenous fishing practices, handed down from one generation to the next for thousands of years, ensured that fish populations remained healthy. They didn't take too many fish from the one area and they didn't catch undersized fish or fish carrying eggs. Apart from fish, Indigenous Australian peoples ate a range of food including yams, berries, shellfish, turtles and large mammals such as kangaroos.

The Murray, South Australia, painted in 1880

Look closely at a $50 note and you will see David Unaipon. Born in 1872, David was a Ngarrindjeri man. As well as being an inventor and author, he was a political activist.

# The Ngurunderi Dreaming

One of the river's best-known animals is the Murray cod. Indigenous peoples say it was a Murray cod that helped form the river. If you were to fly high over the Murray, you would see it curves back and forth, like a wriggling snake.

Some Indigenous peoples who lived along the river say the river's shape was in fact made by a snake. Others say that many years ago, when the river was much smaller, an ancestor named Ngurunderi was chasing an enormous river cod named Ponde. As the fish swam to escape, its giant tail swished back and forth, making the river's curves wide and deep.

This picture of Ponde is carved in rock

## Did you know?

The Murray cod can grow to an incredible size.
The largest Murray cod every recorded was
1.8 metres long and weighed 113 kilograms.

## Europeans arrive

Thanks to the abundance of plants and animals, Indigenous peoples were able to live well on the Murray. But when white Europeans arrived in the 1800s, things changed. European diseases – and the settlers themselves – killed large numbers of Indigenous peoples. Plus, the sheep and cows Europeans brought with them damaged the **native habitats**. It was the beginning of the end for traditional ways of life on the Murray.

Charles Sturt was the first European to travel along the Murray. This drawing from his journal shows the junction of the Darling and Murray rivers.

## Did you know?

The Murray River sustains life for a wide variety of plants such as river red gums. These trees can live for over 700 years. Their large canopies provide shade from the sun, but beware: river red gums can drop their enormous limbs without warning. The branches are big enough to crush cars, as well as people!

# Farming on the Murray

In the late 1800s, European farmers started to grow new crops on farms along the Murray. Because the land along the Murray's banks was dry, the farmers dug **channels** that diverted water from the river to farms and orchards. This was the first time that crops were grown using **irrigation**. It meant that crops that need lots of water, such as cotton and rice, could be grown.

While this change created new opportunities for agriculture, it has come at a cost. One problem is that as water is pulled from the Murray and then used to water crops, salt from **groundwater** seeps back into the river. This extra salt makes the Murray less hospitable to the river's wildlife and less useful for irrigation.

A cotton farm on the Murray River. Cotton was one of the new crops grown by the European farmers.

Irrigation has had a major impact on the flow of the Murray and its sister rivers, as has climate change. Hot, dry weather causes the water levels to drop and can even lead to parts of rivers drying up.

When the drought breaks, heavy rains can swell the rivers and cause them to rise above their banks and flood surrounding land. It's natural for water levels to rise and fall, but recent droughts and floods in the past 20 years have been more severe because of human impact on the climate.

# chapter 3

# How did people travel on the Murray?

Think about a world before trains and cars. Back then, the biggest, fastest and best highways were rivers.

## Bark canoes

Indigenous peoples travelled on the Murray in a canoe called a *yuki*. A *yuki* was made by shaping a single sheet of bark pulled from the giant river red gums that grew alongside the river. Even today, you might be able to spot a gum tree with a large scar from where bark was stripped.

Indigenous people used the bark of the river red gum to make canoes.

The Canoe Tree, Currency Creek, South Australia. The canoe-shaped scar on this tree was created when the bark was stripped to make a canoe.

## Whaling boats

When Europeans first arrived on the Murray in the early 1800s, they navigated the river with oar-powered whaling boats. Unlike canoes, these boats could hold several people at once.

One of the first Europeans to travel the Murray was a British Naval officer named Charles Sturt. He gave the river its English name. With the help of local Indigenous people, Sturt followed the Murray all the way to where it flowed into the Southern Ocean. At the **mouth** of the Murray, he was disappointed to find that it flowed into a series of lakes and shallow lagoons, and that large ships could not pass through to the sea.

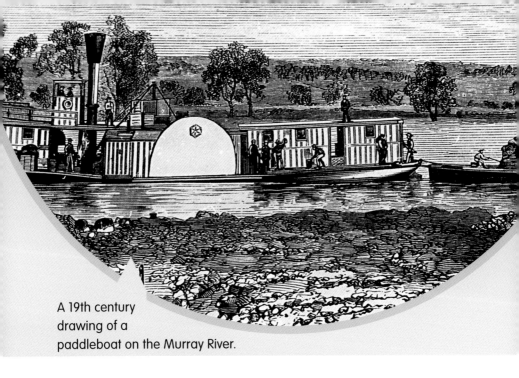

A 19th century drawing of a paddleboat on the Murray River.

## Steam-powered paddleboats

Eventually, white Australians figured out how to bring large boats onto the Murray – steam-powered paddleboats used a giant waterwheel to push the boat through the river. Unlike ocean ships, paddleboats can travel through shallow waters, such as the mouth of the Murray.

In this way, large amounts of people and cargo could easily be transported up and down the river. By the 1860s, there were several companies operating paddleboats on the Murray.

While many boats were used to transport people and goods, other boats were basically floating general stores or even floating churches! At its peak, more than 200 paddleboats were operating on the Murray.

By the middle of the 1900s, transport by trains or trucks replaced most of the Murray's paddleboats. Today, there are still a few paddleboats that carry tourists along the Murray. But you could say travel on the Murray has come full circle: many of the people who boat on the river do so in small kayaks or canoes.

Today, tourists can take a ride on a paddleboat along the Murray River.

# Could the river run dry?

The Murray–Darling Basin is losing its water.  Some of it is drained away to water crops through **irrigation**.  Long droughts brought on by climate change reduce the flow of water into the system.  As less water flows in and more is pulled out, parts of the system are running dry.

Almond trees are grown in dry areas in the Murray–Darling Basin using water from rivers.

# Droughts and floods

Droughts and floods are a normal part of the Murray River system and its sister rivers, like the Darling. But, human activity has made things much worse.

An irrigation channel brings water from the river so cotton can grow.

You can think of the Murray–Darling Basin like a set of buckets on a staircase. Imagine pouring water into the top bucket. The bucket will fill up and, once it is full, water will spill over into the bucket below. This keeps happening down the staircase until all of the buckets are full. The water flows down the stairs, just like a river flows downhill.

A cotton farm, New South Wales. Ninety per cent of Australia's cotton farms are in the Murray–Darling Basin.

## Reduced flow

The Murray and the Darling rivers are just like these buckets. During wet periods, the water flows. During dry periods, less water flows, but there is still water in each bucket, or throughout the river. But if you drain water from the buckets – for irrigation or other uses – water won't flow down the river as easily. And during droughts, the buckets can become completely dry.

That's what has happened on the Darling River. In 2019, whole sections of the river and the surrounding wetlands went dry. Fish and other animals, as well as vegetation, were left without water and died.

Left: A section of the Darling River during a drought. As the flow of water reduces, fish such as the Murray cod (below) can die.

Aerial view of the Murray River wetlands. The Murray River fails to reach the ocean 40 per cent of the time.

This is a problem not just for places on the Darling where the river dries out, but throughout the basin. Any loss of water at the top of the system means that there is less water downstream. What's worse is that people need water most when it is the least available. If it rained all the time, farmers wouldn't need to irrigate their crops and the Murray and Darling would be full of water. But when it's dry, farmers drain water out of the rivers, leaving less water flowing through the system.

# Can we save the Murray?

Making sure water keeps flowing along the Murray and managing who gets the water is a tricky problem.  But there are solutions.  In fact, the Australian Government and the states that rely on the Murray–Darling have put a plan in place.  This plan aims to restore the health of the river system and make sure everyone gets the water they need, including the birds, fish, and other animals and plants that call the Murray home.

The Murray River, South Australia

# Water for everyone

The plan starts with setting limits on how water can be pumped out of the river system. There are also ways to store water so that it is available during droughts. Another part of the plan is to use water more efficiently, so people need less of it.

This means that more water can be put back into the environment and keep the rivers flowing. It's also necessary to recognise the effects of climate change. Climate change has a major impact on the health of the whole system.

**Did you know?**
The Murray and Darling rivers aren't the only bodies of water in trouble. In central Asia, the Aral Sea, once the fourth largest lake in the world, is now less than one-tenth as big as it used to be. That's like If you went from being 1.5 metres tall to standing just 15 centimetres high!

Lake Burrinjuck was created when the Murrumbidgee River was dammed in 1907. It supplies water for towns, irrigated agriculture, industry and the environment.

# Conclusion

If we're not careful, we risk destroying one of the most important natural resources that makes life in Australia possible – the Murray–Darling Basin. It's now up to the Australian people to care for the Murray so it can keep providing for them. This problem is urgent!

The Murray River flows into the Southern Ocean in South Australia. Keeping the river flowing is vital.

# Glossary

**channels** a passage such as a tube through which something flows

**groundwater** water from the earth's surface that has seeped down under the ground and which eventually drains into rivers, lakes or wetlands

**irrigation** the supply of water to crops by artificial means such as pipes and channels

**mouth** where a river flows into the sea

**native habitats** places where animals and plants have lived together for a long time

**navigable** able to be sailed on by a boat

# Index